OASIS

IN THE

HEART

OASIS
IN THE
HEART

❧

Haiku

with

Exposition

By

Toshimi Horiuchi

WEATHERHILL

NEW YORK · TOKYO

First edition, 1995

©1995 by Toshimi Horiuchi

Published by Weatherhill, Inc.
568 Broadway, Suite 705
New York, N.Y. 10012

Printed in the United States.

Library of Congress
Cataloging in Publication Data
Horiuchi, Toshimi, 1931–
    Oasis in the heart: haiku with exposition
/ by Toshimi Horiuchi.
    -- 1st ed.   p.   cm.
    ISBN 0-8348-0330-5
    1. Haiku, American. 2. Nature--Poetry.
    3. Haiku--Authorship.
I. Title.
PR9515.9.H67   1995   95-16057
821--dc20   CIP

To

Dr. Marie Philomène

who has

watched my poetry growing

through the years

CONTENTS

Preface

🌿This collection of haiku represents my work and my reflections upon it over the past twenty years. To each haiku, I have also joined a short exposition.

Critical tradition suggests that a literary work be entirely self-explanatory. However, I have dared to link prose with poetry, feeling that the reader can gain a great deal from this relationship. An exposition, carefully written, can become a part of the poem as well as an explanation of it. It can, therefore, be a valid part of the total experience. I have attempted to represent in my expositions the essential background of each haiku so that my poetry might have a greater effect on the reader's thoughts and feelings.

My haiku was written from observations of nature, from which I attempted to extract beauty and meaning from the very smallest and simplest events of life. A time of special blessing for me is that time which I give to a butterfly, an iris, a lily, a shadow, a cloud, a bird, a fallen leaf, a moon, a rainbow, a cricket, or a snowflake. By attuning my senses to such wonders, I hope to deepen, intensify, and purify my thoughts and feelings, allowing them to relate and interact with each other poetically.

To convey such thoughts and feelings via the short haiku form, I attempted to clarify and simplify my voice as much as possible, so that the imagery might be sharp and penetrating enough to blossom in the reader's mind and heart. It is my hope that through these haiku and expositions both children and adults will learn to relish the reading and writing of haiku.

Acknowledgments

My heartfelt thanks are due to Dr. Marie Philomène, a professor at the Sendai Shirayuri Junior College, who has encouraged me to write poetry through the years; to Sr. Owen Lindblad, a Minnesota writer, who edited the expositions and gave me invaluable suggestions; to Professor Naoshi Koriyama for his appreciative and constructive criticism. Grateful acknowledgment is made to *Poetry Nippon, Frogpond, Kō, The Japan Times,* and *The Mainichi Daily News* for publishing the haiku and essays included in this book. All translations of haiku and *waka* from the Japanese are my own unless otherwise noted.

Introduction

CREATING ENGLISH HAIKU

❧Throughout its development, English poetry has assimilated the poetic forms of other various and distinct cultures. For example, the *sonetto*, invented in Italy in the early thirteenth century, was introduced into English poetry three centuries later. So, too, the haiku, a very old Japanese poetic form, has been accepted as a genre of poetry in the West in the present century. English haiku are formed in three lines, typically totalling seventeen syllables and addressing seasonal topics.

The true poet views the world with keen insight, sees much in little, and feels rapture even in what others might consider trivial or meaningless. Everything discloses something beautiful, something important, or something precious. Thus the eye, the inward eye, plays an important role; one cannot compose poetry unless poetic expressions reflect the observations of this inward eye. To write haiku, one must find truth or beauty in things that others have failed to notice. Therefore, it is absolutely necessary to train the inward eye to discover the poetic elements of everyday life. By focusing a keen eye on things, whether or not visible or tangible, one is able to grasp the poetic reality and crystallize it into a concrete shape.

"Poetry," says Matthew Arnold, "should be simple, sensuous, impassioned." Although haiku is perhaps the shortest poetry, shortness does not imply immaturity or ineffectiveness. Haiku can describe as eloquently as longer poetry can, because the force of haiku lies precisely in its extreme economy of words, with which it weaves poetic worlds of crisp images. The haiku form, then, reflects a philosophy of simplicity, expressing much by saying as little as possible. In appreciating haiku, much is left to the reader's imagination, and a keen appreciation is naturally required of the writer as well.

The most essential element of haiku is the feeling of surprise that figuratively explodes in the reader's mind. The writer of haiku and the reader are linked to each other through this surprise, and the inability to convey it implies that the haiku is not well crafted.

The feeling of surprise in haiku is produced by a combination of beauty, novelty, simplicity, euphony, and lucidity. Beauty is acquired by framing graceful links between things; novelty by initiating new links; simplicity by erasing every suggestion of prose and condensing expression; euphony by creating resonance between words and between lines; and lucidity by eliminating every impurity. All these elements must blend in perfect harmony for the haiku to have the maximum force of surprise.

Now and then a fact or some aspect of reality is contorted or changed to create or increase poetic effect. Destruction of a logical relation between things sometimes creates the great surprise the best haiku conveys. To build a favorite image, the poet sometimes needs to destroy what is apparent or expected in nature and life.

The internal ordering of poetic elements—image structure, meaning structure, and sound structure—must also be considered prudently. The arrangement of lines is important to produce a visual, acoustical, or psychological effect. Punctuation can add poetic rhythm. It is necessary to create an order of words that is most suitable for expressing feelings or thoughts, making the most of every element of language—sound, rhythm, color, aroma, and image. A poet may paint a flower with sound, compose music in color, describe a feeling in scent. Any word which does not serve this purpose should be deleted. A poet must search for that particular word for which no other can substitute—a word wrapped in melodious sound and strong image.

And last but not least is the poetic blank space existing between words, between lines, and at the end of haiku. In such poetic blank space, feeling and thought flow, sound and sense fuse, expanding the poetic afterimage. Without this the soul of haiku lies silent, like seed unexposed to water and sun.

<h2>How to Make English Haiku "Bloom"</h2>

The haiku is a form of "one-point poetry." Accordingly, haiku cannot overcrowd its small vessel with ideas such as a sonnet or blank verse can. Nevertheless, haiku can convey as deep a thought or as intense a feeling as poems of other genres.

As in any other work of art, haiku must contain elements that appeal to the reader's senses and imagination. Haiku has as its core the commonplace. It is from the expression of the ordinary in our lives that the form probably developed. Because haiku sets forth the poetry of everyday experience, both the reading and the writing of it can be enjoyed almost any place, at any time, by anyone.

Words are the instruments used to "play" the poetry existing in the poet's mind just as the strings of a piano are used to play the music imagined in the composer's mind. Haiku poets must arrange these words in such a way that they blend in the small vessel of haiku to yield a perfect poetic reaction, somewhat like a proper combination of chemicals in a scientific study will produce a specific chemical reaction.

One poetic quality of haiku is the novelty or freshness produced when two elements, seemingly unrelated, are linked in a sudden and interesting way. One of these elements may be simply a general condition: an objective description of a state of being, an object, some scenery, or a situation. The other element may be the poet's own perception of the general condition: his or her emotional, intellectual, subjective, or objective apprehension of a truth. Such expressions, however, are not yet poetry. They must be sublimated to extract their essence. Just as wine is the essence of grapes, so poetry is the essence of expressed poetic qualities; as wine will intoxicate, so will poetry move the reader profoundly.

In spite of the careful crafting of the elements of haiku, multiple levels of interpretation are possible, creating room for the reader to fully exercise the senses, the imagination, the intellect, and the spirit, discovering something new to fill the space. Because of this vagueness, understanding haiku is not simply a logical process. For some, thinking illogically is unacceptable because their ways of understanding demand only the reasonableness of a "hard mind." Others, however, are more open to things not easily explained; they understand with a "soft mind." Poetry requires just such a "soft mind" in order to comprehend things beyond the apparent and explicable.

A poet creates in close rapport with nature. The reader, in turn, comprehends the haiku because of his or her close rapport with this form of expression. To commune so closely with nature, a poet must have a "soft mind." Likewise, to relate so intimately with haiku, the reader must have a "soft mind." Without this gift, neither writing nor reading haiku can be fully enjoyed.

To many, haiku may seem easy to write and to read, but it is difficult to create original poetry within the discipline of seventeen syllables. It is not easy to plumb the depths of poetic thought available in haiku. However, reading haiku does sharpen the ability to write it, and writing haiku does sharpen the skills of reading and interpretation.

Zeami (1363–1443), a superb Japanese actor and playwright, speaks of originality in art as a flower. To make this flower "blossom" in the mind, an artist or poet must continually examine his or her own work and add new devices to it. Efforts must always be made to keep creativity fresh and forthright. One must break away from yesterday's thoughts, change one's ways of seeing and thinking, and so be ever recreated in the newness of today and tomorrow. Zeami's words are as insightful today as they were six centuries ago. By them, it is suggested that all artists and haiku poets have within themselves the possibility to continually create "flowers" of genuine and lasting beauty.

SEASON WORDS AS A KEY TO HAIKU

The *Kokinshū* (Collection of Ancient and Modern Poems) is an anthology of *waka,* (an unrhymed Japanese verse form of five lines containing five, seven, five, seven, and seven syllables respectively) compiled and edited in the year 905. The *waka* in this early anthology were divided into four seasonal groups, according to clues they contained indicating the time of year. Ever since, Japanese poets have been selecting, classifying, and refining, these "season words," called *kigo,* according to the seasonal phenomena and regular annual events occurring in Japan.

Thus, consciousness of *kigo* has been fostered throughout the long history of *waka.* In the *waka* contained in the *Kokinshū,* the idea of *kidai* or seasonal themes is clearly evident. *Kidai* were selected according to the aesthetic senses of the poets in the Heian Period (794–1192), and poetry was composed after reflecting upon the harmony existing between nature and humanity. The following *waka* by Ono no Komachi is from the *Kokinshū:*

Hana no iro wa	The cherry flowers
Utsurinikeri na	Whose color faded away,
Itazura ni	While I passed the days
Waga mi yoni furu	Thinking of the world in vain
Nagame seshi ma ni	In the long rainy weather.

A famous poetess of the Heian Period, Komachi in this *waka* feels, as a middle-aged woman, at one with the withered flowers and the long rains. This oneness elicits the expression of her pensive, even sad mood. The withered flowers in particular, which are the *kidai* of this poem, bring into relief the content of the poem.

Waka was a poetic form composed by whole groups of poets. The members of these groups needed a common ground on which to build a mutual understanding of their literary pieces, and they chose the idea of seasonal themes. In fact, they considered *kidai* an essential element to be kept and shared among themselves. Even today, Japanese haiku poets gather monthly or bimonthly to walk meditatively around fields and hills in order to create haiku. These walks are called *ginkō*. At such haiku gatherings, or *kukai*, the poets enjoy reading and appreciating each other's new pieces.

The *kigo* of haiku work in many ways, most importantly as code words to condense poetic expression. A haiku without *kigo* loses compactness and succumbs to the prosaic. Haiku follows this axiom: "The fewer the words, the broader the vista of meaning." Season words provide haiku with tone; that is, intellectual and emotional color to embellish contents. *Kigo* tend to unite and synthesize the elements of words. These elements yield to kaleidoscopic combinations which leap and intertwine among multilayered mutations in the reader's mind. When *kigo* do not work well, they can actually diminish the haiku. Using an English haiku of mine as an example, I will explain these functions of *kigo* more concretely:

a winter fly
embracing
its shadow

One winter day as I sat alone at my desk by the window in my study, a fly resting there attracted my attention. It sat motionless, embracing its shadow cast on the desktop by the sun. Most flies had died by this time, and this one still clung so tenuously to life in the midst of the severe winter that I thought it might die at any moment. I perceived through watching this winter fly insights concerning the final condition of my life. These thoughts deepened, and the fly melted my heart with pity. I gazed for a long while, pondering the little insect.

If the word "winter" is replaced with another, the elements of this haiku will cease functioning harmoniously as poetry. Vestiges will remain but the poem will certainly not be a quality haiku. It would seem possible to use "bee" or "butterfly" in place of a fly, but it was a fly that I saw at the time. Nor can the position of any word in this haiku be changed. If any word is shifted to another place, the haiku will be weaker.

As explained in the exposition provided, the *kigo*, "a winter fly," provokes the emotional response that colors this haiku, supplies a background of imagery, and enriches the haiku's implication or significance. One can find words rich in symbolism or description outside of *kigo*, but the intense effects made by season words in haiku cannot be neglected. Bashō wrote several haiku without *kigo*. These, however, are considered mere jingles, proving that the season words are at the very core of haiku.

Haiku reflects the Japanese traditional sense of beauty which claims priority over objectivity and science. For this reason, some *kigo* do not follow logic. For example, the word, "rainbow" used by itself implies a summer rainbow. Of course, we can also see rainbows at other times, so we then must use a word to indicate which season: a winter rainbow—a rainbow in the winter sky.

Since the characteristic traits of seasons differ from country to country, many *kigo* lack universality. This problem prompts us to consider seriously how *kigo* should be used or changed in English haiku. As English haiku cannot be mere imitations of Japanese haiku, so English haiku poets should not be forced to follow Japanese *kigo*. They must establish a *kigo* that will be more intelligible throughout the English-speaking world, with all its diversity.

As in other forms of poetry, the Japanese haiku form has arisen from the deeply rooted artistic instinct of humankind and the inner necessity of expressing such depths aesthetically. Poetry, in general, as Aristotle observes in his *Poetics,* seems to have sprung from two sources: the instinct for imitation and the instinct for harmony and rhythm.

A Japanese haiku contains seventeen syllables, though the number of syllables in English haiku need not necessarily be the same. The entire poem, however, is to be read in one breath both in English and in Japanese. Haiku is "one-breath poetry," and the number of syllables is closely related to this physical necessity. "One breath" coincides with what is sometimes called the "haiku moment." In this sense, haiku is "momentary" poetry.

The externalization of poetic thought or emotion is closely connected with the form or vehicle that carries it to the reader. One of the important considerations in English verse forms is line division, and here we find an essential difference in the very nature of Japanese and English haiku. Because conventional Japanese haiku is written as one vertical line in a single column, some think the English haiku should also be written in one line and, moreover, that the Japanese haiku should be translated in one line. "One line" or the figure "1" for some symbolizes the essence of simplicity or brevity.

James Kirkup (1923–) writes both one-line haiku and three-line haiku in English, while Hiroaki Satō (1942–) translates haiku into English exactly according to the traditional form of the Japanese haiku. Lafcadio Hearn (1850–1904) arranged Moritake Arakida's (1475–1549) haiku about a butterfly into three lines in Romanized form:

> *Rakka eda ni*
> *Kaeru to mireba*
> *Kocho kana!*

However, Hearn uses the one-line form in his English translation of the poem: "When I saw the fallen flower return to the branch—lo! it was only a butterfly!"

Translated this way, as a single line of sixteen words and twenty-two syllables, the haiku seems rather prosaic and lengthy. English poetry does have a single-metrical-line form called "monostich," which is used for aphorism or epigram. Yet one-line haiku in English can sound monotonous, both visually and acoustically, and some think that one-line English haiku do not look like poems. Besides, the reader or the hearer tends to unconsciously restructure one-line English haiku, especially those that run longer than twelve syllables.

Though transcribed in a one-line form, the most common Japanese haiku exhibit a sound unity or sense unity which contains the very essence of the piece. Conscious of this nuance, Basil Hall Chamberlain (1850–1935) rendered Moritake's poem above into the following English couplet.

Fallen flower returning to the branch;
Behold! It is a butterfy.

The two-line English haiku not only produces a sort of poetic rever-
beration between lines, but also discloses more clearly the unexpected
development that is the hallmark of well-written haiku.

In general, the seventeen syllables of haiku are divided into three
parts, each of which forms a unit to create the required balance of
rhythm. The three parts are derived from the fundamental five seg-
ments composing *waka* or *renga* (linked verse): five, seven, five, seven,
and seven syllables. Haiku originates from the first three segments
called *hokku*. *Waka* poets were more concerned with the number of syl-
lables than line division (although Takuboku Ishikawa (1886–1912)
wrote *tanka* in three lines).

These three segments are separated in three-line haiku, and they
should work just like the three movements (exposition, development,
and climax) of the sonata form or the three acts of the modern play.
The seventeen syllables are arranged into three lines in a five-seven-five
pattern so that they will yield acoustical and visual harmony and sym-
metry. Since the three lines well exhibit the characteristic internal orga-
nization of the Japanese haiku, English dictionaries, almost with one
voice, define haiku as a Japanese verse form comprising three lines.
Neither monostich nor couplet forms give haiku this degree of harmo-
ny and symmetry.

Because there are limits in keeping rhythm or acoustical harmony,
shorter lines are easier for the hearer to "catch" or memorize. They are
easier to recite as well, and thus lines in poetry are generally classified
according to the length of breath as well as the length in feet. On the
other hand, a line in poetry is not necessarily a unit of meaning; in poet-
ry, it is rare for individual lines to constitute complete units of meaning.

The three-line haiku positively embodies the writer's idea of its internal organization. These elements of haiku seem to be the impetus for writing English haiku in triplet form. In Yone Noguchi's book of poetry *The Pilgrimage,* published in London in 1909, there appeared several English haiku in three-line form. Following is my English version of the haiku of Moritake written in three-line form:

> a fallen flower
> returns to the branch alone:
> a butterfly

In this version, the poet first presents the image of flowers fallen on the earth. He then suddenly directs the reader's gaze to one of them that returns to the branch. Surprisingly, the flower becomes a butterfly in flight. By superimposing one image on another, the poet accomplishes a poetic transformation or momentary poetic truth in nature's metamorphoses. This haiku of Moritake consists of three ideas: the thesis (the stillness of fallen flowers on the earth); the antithesis (the movement of a fallen flower returning to the branch); and the synthesis (of the stillness of fallen flowers and the movement of a fluttering butterfly superimposed upon a fallen flower).

As the sonnet varies in form (Italian, Spenserian, Shakespearian, etc.), so can English haiku differ in form (monostich, couplet, triplet). As blank verse gives freedom to English poetry, so does haiku give the English haiku flexibility regarding the number of syllables and lines. It is essential for a poet to experiment with as many forms as possible in order to remain free enough to render his or her poetic experience.

Any verse form should lend clarity to a poet's spiritual insight and enhance the significance of his or her theme. The value of a poem depends on the totality of its poetic thought (the internal) and poetic form (the external). The value of the haiku form depends on how effectively it encourages meaning and interpretation; in the end, it is the writer's intention that decides which form will most aesthetically express the haiku's content.

A Poem a Day Keeps the Doctor Away

It is observed by practitioners of Oriental medicine that the human mind rules the body and that illness indicates a negative state of mind—thoughts dwelling on anger, anxiety, fear, or jealousy. In Shakespeare's *Twelfth Night* (I, iii, 1-3), Sir Toby Belch affirms this view when he says to Maria:

> What a plague means my niece, to take the death of her
> brother thus? I am sure care's an enemy to life.

According to this thinking, one can be cured of an illness by changing negative thoughts to positive ones, brightening a gloomy mind by banishing care. Illnesses of the mind and body have often been cured by charms and incantations of one kind or another since primitive ages. When a human voice blends with the lovely timbre and rhythm flowing from a poem, the poem fascinates, softens, and brightens the mind. In his poem "The Day is Done" American poet Henry Wadsworth Longfellow (1807–82) wrote:

> Come, read to me some poem,
> Some simple and heartfelt lay,
> That shall soothe this restless feeling,
> And banish the thoughts of day.

In ancient Greece, Apollo was considered the god of poetry and music as well as medicine, light, and prophecy. It was believed that poetry was effective in curing diseases. Conjurers charmed away illnesses of the mind and body by chanting magical words. So it appears that poetry took its origin from this source and was used as a most primitive medical treatment as well as being a most instinctive creative activity.

Something like a seed exists in the human body that, when touched by a poetic or beautiful manifestation, germinates, grows, and blooms. A striking example of this influence of incantation upon such a seed is still seen today in the songs and chants of Buddhists, American Indians, Christians, and even rock groups. All are poetry.

There exists in every person an innate creative urge to give form to what does not exist in the external world, to feelings that cannot be grasped by the senses. Poetic creation is one of the activities arising from this instinctive desire. It is in the deep, human, primitive instincts that strong desire resides and continually reaches out toward beauty, which preserves and stimulates a full and vigorous life. We each have within us a restless, lonely soul constantly desiring a lovely flower to bloom, wanting to give birth to a lively spirit. Such a soul is clearly represented in this poem by William Wordsworth (1770–1850):

> My heart leaps up when I behold
> A rainbow in the sky:
> So was it when my life began;
> So is it now I am a man;
> So be it when I shall grow old
> Or let me die!

This poem resounds from the depths of the poet's soul, which desires to behold this thing of beauty, this rainbow, forever. Every human heart shakes with deep emotion when it encounters a truly beautiful thing. "Beauty," as John Keats reminds us, "is a joy forever."

How are we to approach such beauty? I believe we can approach a world where beauty does exist, not through scientifically precise ways, but through the natural harmony already existing between the objective and subjective eye, between feeling and intellect. We think more deeply and see more precisely when our emotions are engaged. Intellect and emotion complement one another.

The creative poetic power that exists in this framework is further enriched and strengthened by freeing the mind from every other thing, from every restraint, so that it may play with abandon. By responding to the call from the depths of a thing visible or invisible, the creative mind is drawn into a profound world of beauty and wonderment, and out of this world is woven the language of poetry.

Freed from commonplace use, words in poetry assume a vivid life of their own. Acutely refined, they take on metaphysical dimensions (that is, subtle emotions embracing both the spiritual and intellectual). Tinged with these fresh meanings and cadences, words shine within the fabric of a poem, but unless words have such luminosity and originality in themselves, the poetry will fade and die. The following lines by C. D. Lewis, from his *Poetry for You*, bask in the brilliant aura of their words:

> Autumn leaves are falling
> like a snowstorm on fire.

"Snowstorm" here reflects the movement and profusion of autumn leaves as the wind blows them down from the trees, while the word "fire" reflects their color. All the words work together to exactly express the falling autumn leaves that the writer sees with his own eyes. All nine words were chosen and arranged most effectively to reveal the imagery the writer intended. "Autumn leaves are falling" is a description based on the poet's objective eye, while "like a snowstorm on fire" reveals his subjective eye.

Poetic words secrete ever-new meanings, sounds, and rhythms in order to move human sensibilities. The words originate in the mind but flow through the human body. We must meet the desires of body and spirit with both bread and word. In this way, poetic words form a kind of communion among people. The harmonious blend of word and poetic ambience creates beauty.

A good haiku has something of an incantatory charm to store up spiritual and emotional energy in the human system. Haiku tends to create a ground on which all human suffering melts away—loneliness, anxiety, uneasiness, sorrow, illness, pain, and so on. Haiku shifts the mind from darkness to light. It opens the door for the natural expression of self. Haiku's many functions serve to strengthen the natural healing powers within and to activate life.

In such a way, this haiku crystallized in itself that imagery which is most connected with primitive joy or pleasure. This is something that science cannot explain. For example, a scientific mind would be unable to represent a scene like this:

> morning rain
> taps on trees:
> bud, bud, bud . . .

The poet, Santōka Taneda (1882–1949), was a man who lived with haiku. Santōka had encountered various sufferings from early childhood: his father was a drunk and a libertine; his mother committed suicide when he was eleven; he himself failed in marriage and tried to commit suicide. So, as a mendicant monk, Santōka became a wanderer and wrote haiku.

> muddy water flows
> making clear itself

Santōka's wanderings became a journey into the depths of the human heart. He poured haiku into the cup of his soul; saké into the cup of his body. Haiku became Santōka's very life.

Erich Kästner (1899–1974) published a collection of his own poems under the title *Doktor Erich Kästner's Lyrische Hausapotheke* (Lyrical Home Remedies) in 1936. In this book, Kästner arranges his poems so that each of them might work effectively upon the reader like medicine that doctors give patients, according to the condition of their illnesses. In his book *The Poet's Way of Knowledge* (1957), Cecil Day Lewis (1904–72) states simply: "A poem a day keeps the psychiatrist away." In 1990, several members of the Arts Therapy Society of Japan published a book entitled *Haiku Renku Therapy* (Sogen-sha Press, Osaka, Japan). This book reports that haiku therapy has done commendable work healing mental diseases in Japan. Today, haiku therapy is a recognized branch of arts therapy and a useful tool in psychotherapy.

Although tiny in form, the haiku is as piquant as a pepper pod. It has dispelled the gloom of mind and heart and healed the sick. Thirsting souls are quenched by the pure water that flows naturally from the spring of the everyday poetic mind. In this highly civilized and technological society, haiku, which is the poetry of the ordinary, the natural, and the everyday shall continue to play its role as a good physician.

OASIS
IN THE
HEART

thawing icicles:

moonlight falls

in drops

◗THE MOON shines brightly on ici-
cles hanging from the eaves. A sense
of spring is evident, and delicate fra-
grances float in the darkness. The
icicles melt in drops of moonlight,
which fall slowly and rhythmically to
the ground, break into pieces, and
vanish into the earth. This dramatic
finale to winter continues through-
out the night. Frozen forms return
to their origin at the bidding of the
new season. In this way, new vistas of
beauty are molded, flowers are
opened, and the earth is clothed
again in a carpet of green.

thawing icicles:

moonlight falls

in drops

◗A SNOWSTORM has passed through.
The morning sun makes all the earth
dazzlingly white, all the skies daz-
zlingly blue. A completely white
world lies around me. Nothing
moves, nothing sounds. All is frozen
in whiteness. Then, on a white lake
ahead of me, a single point begins to
move. A piece of the whiteness, a
swan lifting in flight, becomes air-
borne. Several more "launchings"
follow. Life is breathing once again
in the frozen white world.

a piece of white

separates from whiteness:

a parting swan

alps upon alps—

vanishing snows

expose greening verdure

THE BLUE SKY seems limitless, the earth appears multicolored, and birds fill the air with their song. Off in the distance, a range of mountains cluster, one tumbling over another. The snows on these mountains have melted and a carpet of rich, green vegetation flourishes in their place.

Sometimes we stay too close to the things we are viewing and cannot really see them clearly. So it is good to distance ourselves at times. A long distance provides us with other kinds of beauty—like snow on mountains melting into green vibrancy.

THE STILLNESS of the evening invites me outdoors, and I go for a walk around the pond. A crescent moon is piercing the darkening sky, and the air hangs motionless as if there were nothing breathing. But a goldfish is swimming in the pond, causing little ripples on the water. The fish bites at the reflection of the moon again and again. The bobbing crescent breaks apart but very quickly gathers itself together again.

a goldfish

is biting

a crescent moon

AT MIDNIGHT in the hospital, most patients seem to be asleep. No sound is heard except the chirping of a cricket coming, so it seems to me, right through the concrete walls. It disturbs me. All night long I wonder why the cricket is singing and what it is telling me. I listen until its voice is finally drowned in the onrush of morning noises.

in dead of night

a cricket's voice squeezes

through the concrete wall

a cricket's voice

ripples the darkness

thinned by moonlight

❧ONE DAY, numberless crickets chirped harmoniously together in the grass. But tonight, a single cricket's voice ripples the sea of silence as though for the repose of the departed ones or to call out to the silence. The moon consoles the cricket by casting its pale light over the darkness. The cricket's voice finally loses life but not before it is raised to the highest pitch possible in a last outpouring of song.

cherry blossoms

are falling with flakes

of moonlight

❧THE LIGHT of the full moon is falling over a woodland. Cherry blossoms past their prime are quietly fluttering down. They appear like flakes of moonlight. The sight is one of profound and absorbing beauty. Thus it is that by combining certain elements—moonlight fluttering in flakes—a more perfect form of esoteric beauty is created.

THE GARDEN is still covered with snow, but the warm sunshine, which had lost its power during the cold winter, is now accelerating in intensity. The snow begins to soften, break, and melt. The water soaks into the warming earth. Several stones reveal their dark forms above the melting snow, and grow steadily larger like bamboo shoots. The sure step of spring loosens the hardened world, paints discolored things, perfumes scentless things, awakens sleeping things, and revives lifeless things. All the earth responds to the thaw of a warm spring sun.

melting snow:

garden stones

are growing

MIZUBASHŌ, skunk cabbage, is a wild flower without a stalk, that grows gregariously in swamps in the northern districts of Japan. The plant puts out a handled inflorescence about twenty inches long just after the thawing of the snows. Then a sharp, white elliptical bud opens and blossoms into a light-green flower in a sheath. The plant, as a whole, resembles a white flame or a plume of water.

the incarnation

of melted snow?

mizubashō

silence in silence

to a butterfly's voice

a poppy is nodding

THE MIDDAY SKY is cloudless, the air creamy. Not a breeze stirs. In the silence, so lucid that a butterfly's voice can be heard, poppies stand quietly in bloom. A single one attracts my attention. A butterfly has lighted on the poppy and is tenderly whispering to it. The poppy responds with a very slight nod to the butterfly. Everything is as it should be for such a mysterious, lovely interlude.

silence in silence:

to a butterfly's voice

a poppy is nodding

IT IS SUMMER in the northern country. Fields, hills, and mountains are clothed in green. Flowers bloom profusely and showers have refreshed all the growing things as well as the air itself. All of nature expands in beauty under a life-giving sun. Even the butterflies are dancing, by twos and threes, in time to birdsong from the woods. I stop on the wayside to watch a butterfly frolic around me. But in an instant, it is gone, leaving behind a soft scent of lavender. I shall never meet that butterfly again.

a butterfly

passes by—

lavender scent

on fallen leaves

my shadow rustles—

silence behind

❧IN THE CHILLY SUNSHINE of a late autumn day, the lake glitters, reflecting cobalt blue from the sky above. Tall white birches, oaks, and maples stand guard around the lake. Their leaves are falling and the trees look quite naked. Not even birds visit these trees bereft of their summer finery. I am walking with my shadow. It touches the fallen leaves along the pathway, making a dry, crunching sound as their withered lives are crushed out. Deep silence remains. The season is quickly turning to winter.

an evening calm:

golden slices merge

into a full moon

❧EVENING BREEZES have softened. Ruffled waters on the lake have quieted. Now golden bits and pieces scattered about the lake flock together, composing themselves into a full moon. This moon in the water encourages the lake to echo with a golden light, well-blended with the moon in the night sky. The evening calmness gleams on the lake and in my mind as well.

AFTER THE SNOWSTORM, fields lie silent. Whiteness stretches to the horizon. Where have those cries of wind and cold gone? Yesterday's world is nowhere to be found today. Rather, the peaceful, white earth is playing a winter symphony under the blue sky in order to soothe the injuries and torment of the previous day's tempest.

silence resounds whiteness;

whiteness resounds blue—

a winter symphony

DAPHNE FLOWERS open in early spring, banishing the winter with their sweet smell. This evening, the moon is blooming high in the sky. Gently warming moonlight touches the daphne flowers, swelling their scent. The air, too, is softened in the fragrant moonlight. These flowers are telling the sleeping world to wake up. Into my ears comes the throbbing of the earth.

daphne flowers:

moonlight swells

their fragrance

splendorous morning:

sunbeams gather

on cherry blossoms

❧A BUSH WARBLER'S SONG causes me to open my window. The morning air is fresh and clear and I gaze out over the scene before me. A hill some distance away attracts my particular attention. Sunlight has gathered on the blossoms of cherry trees growing in a grove of pine trees. The delicate beauty of the blossoms is intensified by the dark green of the pines. This event takes place during spring's climactic unfolding when the petals of many other flowers are dropping as though unable to bear the weight of the sunlight.

◢UNDER A STARLESS SKY, the darkness of night deepens. The heat of the day softens. Presently, the glow of a single firefly blinks on and off. Other fireflies still seem to be sleeping under the leaves. Then, the faintest sound imaginable arises out of the stillness. I listen intently and stare wide-eyed with wonder into the darkness. Each time the little firefly lights up, the darkness itself flows directly toward it. I wonder, is it the goal of the darkness to extinguish this brief, beautiful firefly glow?

toward the glow

of a firefly

darkness surges

◢THE DREARY GARDEN shows no sign of its past productive life. An accompanying darkening atmosphere yields no sound but the feeble efforts of a solitary cricket calling to the silence. Its call goes unheeded. The cricket alone lives, but this may well be its last day on earth. Sensing this pitiable end, the cricket cries out to the silence. Or perhaps it is singing a requiem for all the departed souls.

dusky field:

a cricket calling

to the silence

a tulip

is open

like a smile

❧AT THE ROADSIDE, a tulip smiles up at me. Immediately, my morning is brightened and I break out into a smile myself. I repeat the words again and again: "A tulip is open like a smile." At this, a little tune fitting the words forms in my mind. I hum the tune over and over and sing the words to myself. This melodious song bathes my passage through the day.

insect voices

trail off:

barren silence

❧THERE WAS NO SOUND on earth except the voices of insects singing under the clear evening sky. Soon clouds gathered, however, to extinguish the stars and darken the sky. Insect voices faded to nothing in the heavy blackness. The silence that followed was strangely empty. I walked on alone into the dawn in this void that hung about me.

EVENING CHURCH BELLS have stopped ringing. Their sound fades away into a nearby forest as silence is renewed. The scent of lilac drifts out of the stillness and touches the after-image of the ringing bells. This spring day passes peacefully into night. So it is that poetry often exists in some momentary phenomenon seen between things.

the dying sound

of church bells—

scent of lilac

at dusk

peonies fold

sunlight

⚘PEONIES are particularly fascinating to me and speak to my innermost heart. Because they open fully in the fresh air and sunlight, they seem to me to be actually made of sunlight. Their petals are very thin, transparent, and spritely. In the evening when the peonies close, they seem to fold in the sunlight only to burst out and bloom again as sunlight the next day.

at dusk

peonies fold

sunlight

⚘THE HAY is drying in the sun. Beside sleeping cows people rest in the shade of leafy trees, their faces streaming with beads of sweat. The air does not move. Bees do not show themselves. Even vegetables have stopped breathing. Sunflowers, once so vigorous, stand still in the arid fields under the burning sun as if they were offering prayers for rain.

beads of sweat—

sunflowers

stand still

a lily

in a vase:

stillness within stillness

🖙A SLENDER VASE holds a single lily motionless. The two objects are silhouetted against the wall of a room, distinct, yet harmoniously interacting with each other. Nothing moves or breaks the silence that encompasses them. Stillness is superimposed upon stillness, silence upon silence, until the lily becomes itself a visible stillness. Both flower and vase reflect a unity whose beauty is stillness within stillness, silence within silence.

the spring sun—

little eyes shine

on branches

🖙NATURE IS FULL of whims, changeable and uncertain. But now, surely, the winter is far away. Its power cannot reach the sun any more. Knowing this, vegetables push up tender shoots from the earth. Small buds on branches shine like eyes as nature expresses its joy everywhere. Even buds of joy swell in human hearts. Spring is the mother of joy.

❧EARLY SPRING seems to have a cycle of warm days and cold days. It is entirely unpredictable. Yesterday I saw spring in the fields and the woods; I scented spring on the wind. This morning my breath appears as white puffs on the frosty air. The day is calm but sprouting willows lining the street tremble in the cool sunshine. In this northern country, spring advances and retreats like a flirtatious suitor.

spring sunshine:

sprouting willows tremble

in the shivering air

❧IT WAS IN my forty-ninth year that I obtained admission to Saint John's University in Collegeville, Minnesota. The bud of my long-cherished dream as a poet burst forth in the spring sunshine. It became the most significant spring of my life. I studied there for two years.

Several years have passed since my return home. But those hours spent at Saint John's University have crystallized for me into the image of a precious jewel. Even now, when spring comes around, I remember that great joy vividly, and the brilliance of the jewel ripples within me.

the spring sun:

a brilliant jewel

ripples within me

chill in spring—

warmed by familiar voices

on the phone

❧APRIL IN JAPAN is the time to transfer to new offices or schools. It is also the time to enter companies or schools for the first time. It always takes us some time to adjust to these new circumstances and places. In addition, even the springlike weather can be deceiving and the wintry cold return to stir our lonely minds. At such times, our hearts are warmed and encouraged by the familiar voice of a parent or friend coming to us over the telephone.

the breeze

twines

around roses

❧BRIGHTNESS COVERS the garden. A faint breeze blows and stirs the leaves and petals of blazing red roses. Their sweet fragrance colors the morning air. I step up to the roses and feel the breeze twine around them like a scarf of silk. The sun sweetens them more just as they sweeten the breeze with their fragrance. And the breeze, in turn, enlivens all of the garden. Some voice asks, "What can you do for this garden?" My thorny answer to this question pierces the nerves of my mind.

❧MORNING GLORIES are very frail. They bloom just before daybreak and droop in the first sunshine. They cannot stand warmth or brightness. I also think they are unable to stand a noisy world. What they do love may be only a single beautiful moment in this world. That one moment of expression is in the quiet glimmer of predawn light. That is why I peruse morning glories just when the first sunshine of day touches them.

city noises—

the morning glory withers

in the first sunshine

❧THE MAPLE TREE standing in the backyard is tinted gold. It shakes itself in the bright setting sun, sometimes gently, sometimes violently, scattering leaves everywhere. The tree soon looks quite naked. It seems to shed itself unsparingly of everything except what is essential for enduring the coming winter.

a maple tree

shakes itself,

scattering golden leaves

touching

the incense

poppies fall

❧MANY FRIENDS gather to offer condolences at her funeral service. Incense burns in front of the household Buddhist altar. Several priests chant sutras in the quiet atmosphere. Smoke from the incense curls slowly about. It touches the petals of poppies which she loved very much. The petals flutter down like dead leaves to the earth. Grief moves her friends to tears. Their sobbing only intensifies the funereal silence.

morning glory—

the dawning noises

disturb the petals

❧JUST BEFORE the breath of night ceases, morning glories start to open. The purest sunshine soaks into their petals. But as the eastern sky brightens, city-noises increase. The sunlight becomes flecked with sound and dirt; the petals of the morning glories quiver softly. Then the rays of the sun lose their purity altogether and the morning glories fade.

As the air grows colder, ivy creeping along a wall withers and changes into its fall colors. The evening sun throws a heatless light on to the wall, surrounding the scene with more desolate aura. The chilly air of this dying season appeals to our tactile sense; the fading and drying of the ivy, to our visual sense.

> *withering ivy:*
>
> *evening sunlight*
>
> *fades on the wall*

It was unusually warm and mild for November. I felt some kind of radiance reflected in the atmosphere. So I walked in the morning garden only to discover rose buds beginning to open on a late-blooming bush. The plant had not ceased to produce flowers throughout the cool days of fall. Though held tightly within, the lateness of the season could not withhold certain beauties.

> *Indian summer:*
>
> *roses burst forth*
>
> *out of radiance*

green fields:

two white butterflies

become one

❧IT IS SPRINGTIME. All is in full bloom. Nature conducts a symphonic exhibit of birds and butterflies, flowers, grasses, trees, and sun-filled skies. Within this harmony of colors and light, a green field becomes the backdrop for fluttering, white butterflies enjoying the blessings of springtime. As I gaze, one butterfly suddenly becomes two; then two become one. The joy of spring rises on luminous wings of love, and peace embraces the whole earth.

green fields:

two white butterflies

become one

❧LEAVES OF GRASS stand motionless in the silent sunshine. A dragonfly is lying down on the ground with its eyes open. It may be listening to a voice from the heart of the earth. Human ears cannot catch this voice but imagination can. The voice carries a message sent by the darkness below to the brightness above. Soon the dragonfly will warm the message in the sun and fly about giving it to the brightness.

a dragonfly

listens to a voice

from the heart of the earth

under the weight

of darkness

a firefly glows

THE AIR does not move. It hangs heavily like a blanket in the night. Somewhere, water runs with refreshing vibrancy. No light is seen except that of the little fireflies, glowing in the dark. Some flicker at the bottom of the darkness; others flutter about in the heavy air, each held there for the barest moment to illuminate one point of darkness. Fireflies present a night fantasy but they perish with the first streaks of dawn.

fluttering wings:

a moth is caught

in starlight

THE NIGHT SKIES are serene and the stars brightly glow as I stroll casually along a garden path. Suddenly, I hear the sound of gently flapping wings. What wings could these be? I wonder. Then I see. A white moth has become intertwined with a thread of starlight. The small creature is writhing to free itself. It is a charged moment.

TOWARD THE END of November, evenings turn chilly. Chirping insects decrease in number. A kind of desolation grows rapidly throughout all nature. Silence deepens, widening its vistas. This evening, only one cricket chirps around me, its voice rippling forlornly across the vast sea of gloomy silence. It is trying bravely, in its own way, to impregnate this immense world with its small life.

sea of silence:

a cricket

ripples

I WAS WALKING ALONE along a path leading to the lake, dragging my shadow beside me. The weather was warm enough to make me perspire and feel a little tired. Suddenly, I saw another shadow swaying along with mine. It was a butterfly. "How has this butterfly come so far after such cold winter days?" I wondered. The fragile insect seemed to be wringing out its last drops of life. I thought, "This butterfly, too, is lonely."

a shadow quivers

beside my own—

a winter butterfly

parting:

a butterfly

follows me

❧THE DAY HAS COME at last when I must return home to Japan from Saint John's University in Minnesota. My two years of study are over. One month has passed since the spring semester ended. My friends have already gone. On this morning in early June, sunlight speckles the campus lawns. No one is around. I begin to walk alone along the lakeside toward the bus stop. I murmur to myself, "When can I be here again?"

Little birds respond in song from the woods. Trees and grass seem to speak to me. Even the water is whispering something. A chipmunk gazes up at me dubiously. The blue of sky and lake resounds softly within me. Then I am conscious of a faint fluttering of wings. I cast a hasty glance behind. A butterfly is following me.

LAST NIGHT, only one cricket sang under the cloudy sky to shake my mind. Tonight, two sing together, quieting my mind. As their voices rise sweetly, the night silence grows clear and distinct. Coolness purifies the starlight. The two crickets become as one as their souls touch. Their song greatly affects all things under the star-studded sky. What a difference these two voices make!

tonight

two crickets

are singing

a winter fly

embracing

its shadow

ONE WINTER DAY as I sat alone at my desk by the window in my study, a fly, also resting there, attracted my attention. It sat motionless, embracing its shadow cast on the desktop by the sun. Most of the flies had died by this time, but this one still clung so tenuously to life in the midst of the severe winter that I thought it might die at any moment. I perceived through watching this winter fly insights concerning the final condition of my life. These thoughts deepened, and the fly melted my heart with pity. I gazed for a long while, pondering the little insect.

a winter fly

embracing

its shadow

ALL FROZEN THINGS on earth have melted in the spring sunshine. Water tumbles freely over a rocky cliff, painting a rainbow in the mist-strewn air. Life itself seems to flow anew in the sunlight pouring through the trees. Water, light, and air; trees, grasses, and animal life all quicken with energy as the earth regenerates and is beautified once again.

melted water

cascades

in a rainbow

into the darkness

grasses release

fireflies

❧THE INTENSITY of a bright summer day is supplanted by the deep black of night. Leaves of grass are aware of this contrast and release fireflies into the darkness to illuminate the furthest recesses of night with their tiny lamps. Perceiving this, the darkness adjusts to these bits of darting light and a new charm suffuses the summer night.

the shower is gone

unfolding over the lake

a scarf of rainbow

❧THE CALM of a summer day is broken with the rising of a wind over the lake. Trees shake themselves; little waves erupt on the water. Sudden lightning provokes a clap of thunder which in turn recalls the lightning. Together, these two forces have summoned heavy clouds from a distance for a downpour of cool rain. With the stage set for the performance, lightning and thunder play out their roles with great gusto. A two-hour matinee runs its course. At the finale, a rainbow is unfolded across the stage and all returns to normal.

It is late afternoon. A rain has just passed over. I open the window to see the world after the refreshing shower. The air feels cool and the wind has dropped. The sky has brightened. Sparrows cheerfully chatter in the bamboo grove. . . . Suddenly, they stop. Silence. Then, a rainbow! Its colors create a brilliant arch in the sky. This beautiful moment fascinates even the sparrows. Surely, it will move every earnest soul.

a rainbow—

sparrows stop

chirping

Summertime is approaching its zenith. Peonies bloom gloriously under the midday sun. A butterfly nearly touches the flowers with its quivering wings. The peonies respond with quivering petals. Both butterfly and peonies beam ecstatically as they brush each other's beauty. The butterfly becomes sweeter; the peonies magnify grace. In this way, love and beauty flourish in perfect harmony in the summer sunshine.

in midday sun—

a butterfly quivers

over peonies

a morning lake—

wagtail touches

a rainbow

IN A PLACID SUMMER SKY, a rainbow hangs in full bloom over the lake. It is morning. A wagtail on a rock by the shore looks down at the water, jerking its long tail up and down. Then the lovely bird takes wing, skimming the surface of the lake, touching the reflection of the rainbow. After its short excursion, the wagtail returns to the rock. The image of the brilliant-colored rainbow flickers softly on the water. All of nature is at peace. An earlier storm has synthesized all the natural elements so that now the rainbow in the sky shines harmoniously with the one in the water. This perfect duo of rainbows fills my senses with deep pleasure.

a morning lake—

wagtail touches

a rainbow

on leaves of grass

the season fades away

with insect cries

●Most of the leaves have turned to autumn shades of reds, browns, yellows, and grays. The number of singing insects have dwindled and their voices are more subdued. All of nature blends and softens, quiets itself, and sheds its outer beauty as late autumn days turn to winter. It is a time of intense transformation; a silencing of many voices.

withering leaves—

I walk

upon their voices

●The sun's life-giving powers are weakening. Everywhere nature is changing its form and color and sound. Green leaves are losing life and turning thin and brown. Frost has nipped the last brave flowers of the season and ushered in colder temperatures. The scene is one of abandonment and desolation. What I am stepping upon are the dry voices of aging leaves. As I find my own voice in theirs, they also find theirs in mine.

I AM ILL IN BED. The room has a shoji, or paper partition. I cannot see anything outside the house, but I know the wind is blowing by the sound of rustling leaves and the shaking shadows cast on the shoji. As I look at these shadows, they begin to fall in twos and threes. Then the shadows cast in my mind also begin to shake.

rustling leaves—

their shadows on a shoji

fall away

LEAVES FALL from the gingko trees, one after another. They appear to veil the setting sun as they spread through the glowing air, turning a brilliant gold in the autumn sunset. This event is the highlight of the evening. It seems the gingko trees and the western sky are uniting in playing out the finale to a departing season.

gingko trees:

falling leaves

veil the setting sun

a falling leaf

touches the moon's reflection

and my own

A LEAF FELL to the water just in front of me. It fell so silently that not a sound was heard. The moon's reflection and my own trembled together on the water as the leaf touched the surface. The reflections converged, and after several minutes, overlapped. How fragile and how sensitive reflections are! This was the first fallen leaf I saw in the autumn.

chilly sunset:

leaves in flame

chase the wind

TREES BATHE in the evening sun; leaves are aflame under a sky set ablaze with autumn color. The wind enters one sunny woodland after another, rushes about, and deprives the trees of their pleasant warmth. But the wind shivers with cold, too, and shakes the trees. Glowing leaves are suddenly set free. They fly off in droves, chasing the wind with a freezing shout.

THE SUN HAS SET but the sky fringing the mountaintops is still pink. This afterglow fades quickly, and, like embers crumbling suddenly into cold ash, the last drop of ruddy glow falls behind the mountains. Simultaneously, fragile threads holding withered leaves to the branches of trees, are severed by this sudden descent and drop their burdens to the ground.

afterglow

drops—

a shower of withered leaves

IN AUTUMN, trees change into their autumnal dress. The colors of their leaves vary from day to day in richness and depth. Almost every afternoon the woods lures me out. As I walk among the trees, they gift me generously with their abundance of colored leaves. Nature, so plentiful in beauty, soothes my soul and leads me to the essence of being.

when I pass,

trees shower me

with colored leaves

autumn sky

swallows

a rainbow

❧THE RAIN has stopped. Clouds have dispersed and the wind has weakened. A certain brightness hovers on the air as transient raindrops continue to glisten on the leaves. Suddenly, a rainbow breaks through the sky, spreading its color harmony over the autumn earth. Before long, however, I notice the sky has swallowed the rainbow, leaving a distilled blue to tint the heavens. As I gaze, the rainbow still appears to bloom on the other side of the sky. Such natural phenomena form images of great beauty in my mind.

autumn leaves—

the water

on fire

❧BIRCHES, oaks, and maples surrounding the lake are quickly changing color to play out their role in autumn's brilliant drama. Golds and browns, yellows and reds shimmer and dance on the water, creating a kaleidoscopic composition. The sky, too, adds shifting tones of blues and whites to this waterscape. Indeed, trees and sky and water are one in this final display of autumnal glory.

THE FLOWERS have all withered away in the frosty garden. But they continue to bloom within me. I become keenly aware of this fact as I ponder the winter garden. Things of beauty may perish around me but never in my inmost being, where they have an everlasting aspect to their existence. It seems to me that every human being has a soul to sense this.

a winter garden:

beauty blossoms

in memories

YESTERDAY THE SKY was overladen with heavy clouds, the wind raged violently, rain fell in torrents. My mind was in just such turmoil itself. But today, the morning after, the air flows fresh and peaceful. The huge arc of a rainbow hangs serenely before the verdant mountains. My yesterday's sky has cleared and melted into the heart of today's rainbow.

a morning rainbow—

yesterday's sky

blooms serene

the last drop

of wine holds

a moon

It is early one autumn evening. I am sitting alone on a chair in the garden drinking a glass of wine to relieve my fatigue. Moonlight is lulling all things into quiet rest. A light breeze refreshes my dull spirit; the wine quenches my thirsty passion. I casually gaze down into my glass, and there see the moon wavering in the last drop of wine. I observe that such a tiny drop has become a mirror to reflect the real image of a much larger object; and this image reflected in such a tiny thing has power to touch the depths of the human soul.

the last drop

of wine holds

a moon

It is the night of December thirty-first. The temple bells ring out the old year and ring in the new. I toast this New Year with my family and indulge in reminiscing. While I let bygones be bygones, a variety of memories come before my eyes like a colorful kaleidoscope and blend with the wine in my fragile glass. The mixture slightly intoxicates me.

New Year's Eve:

my glass fills

with the wine of memory

calm winter evening:

a fishing boat returns

laden with sun

🖝A FISHING VILLAGE along a small bay is basking in the setting sun. The glow echoes across the sea, while gulls fly about in the chilly air. Cool waters wash the sandy shore with chattering voices. A woman and a child stand gazing out across the sea at a distant speck gradually growing larger and larger. It is a fishing boat, laden with the sun's last light that approaches the inlet. A fisherman is waving his hand and smiling.

the snowy path—

under foot crackles

the moonlight

🖝THE THERMOMETER reads 30 degrees below zero. Everything is frozen, but a full moon beckons me outdoors where the frosty air bites and nips at my skin. Still, the moonlight is so alluring. I step slowly along a snowy path in a nearby woods. I am surprised to hear the moonlight crack and break under my feet. The sound is extraordinarily beautiful. I think perhaps it is the music made by winter itself on the coldest of nights.

❧WINTERS IN MINNESOTA are usually long and severe. It was at the age of fifty that I entered Saint John's University at Collegeville in the heart of Minnesota. Summer had already gone; the leaves of the maples and oaks and birches were turning gold and flaming red. Day and night I devoted myself to the study of poetry and creative writing. Suddenly, it was bitter winter but my soul blazed brighter than ever! In fact, the two years I spent studying and writing in Minnesota were the most fruitful in my life. A dream I had cherished for so long bloomed and flourished and bore much fruit. Indeed, life is a prelude until the age of fifty.

Minnesota!

my fiftieth winter

blazes bright

daffodils:

a drifting cloudlet

shakes the petals

❧WINTER LINGERS. But sweet fragrances are adrift on warmer breezes, and the tender shoots of young plants sprout bravely. A grassy field is already adorned with yellow daffodils made more brilliant by their overlay on so green a carpet. Small white clouds dot the blue sky. Green and yellow, white and blue. Earth blends with sky as the small cloud shadows dip and touch the daffodils, softly ruffling their petals.

after hugging the moon

a spring cloud

retreats

❧THE MOON lies in the middle of a velvety spring sky. Suddenly, a cloud arrives to embrace the moon. The cloud gleams with brief and subtle luminosity. Then, as the wispy intruder floats away, the moon regains its splendor. The cloudless sky brightens and the air stills. Twinkling stars surround the moon. A warmth is felt in the moonlight as again all visible things stir my imagination.

As DUSK GATHERS, I hear someone playing the piano. Moonlight ruffles the surface of a nearby pond studded with water lilies like the star-filled sky. The lilies close with nightfall, wrapping themselves in the moonlight, petal by petal. But their fragrance diffuses and lingers long on the musical cadences of the piano, embellished as well with soothing moonlight.

water lilies

enfold themselves

in moonlight

DARKNESS THICKENS and stills the night air already perfumed with lotus blossoms. No sound but my footstep in the coolness drifts around the pond. Suddenly, for a moment, the dark clouds part and moonlight floods the pond, highlighting the beautiful lotus flowers. That single moment opens a dreamworld of beauty, relieving my mental fatigue.

a break in clouds:

moonlight falls

on lotus flowers

midday heat:

under the water

white clouds lie

🖎AT MIDDAY, the sun is scorching, the air motionless, and the ground dry. Trees and grasses are drooping and even the birds do not show themselves. Beads of perspiration stand out on the foreheads of people in the sun. Unrelenting heat beats down upon the languid waters of a lake. Above, even clouds have lost their power to move. Some have laid their shadows down in repose on a meadow; others lay themselves under the water.

cloud's shadow

shakes a hill

of cosmos flowers

🖎A CLOUD overshadows a hill covered with cosmos flowers. At this touch, both the delicate flowers and the hill shake nervously. They lose their composure. It seems they are trying to shake off the shadow. When the cloud leaves, and its lingering tone fades away, the hill shines once more in the afternoon sun; the cosmos regain their beauty.

IN AN INSTANT, it seemed, as I walked through the night, a great cloud disappeared. Bright moonlight caught at my mind. Joy replaced sorrow. I was very pleased with the moon. "As long as I walk along this way on earth," I thought, "I may see this beautiful creature, the moon." As a night wayfarer, I was greatly encouraged at this and felt my fragile spirit supported. The light in this darkness seemed even more fascinating than the light in the day.

the cloud is gone:

bathing in the moonlight

I walk along my way

EARLY ONE EVENING, a soul departs. A single cricket is singing, deepening the silence. Gradually, other crickets stir and respond. There must be some implicit understanding between them, for they sing together in the withering grass so furiously that it is possible their voices will reach the departing soul. The crickets know that they, too, shall not be on this earth much longer.

a departing soul:

the cricket's song awakens

a chorus of comrades

the winter lake:

a white cloud

touches my hair

❧IT IS WINTER. The lake is very clear. Reflections in the icy water look more beautiful than their realities. I think that at this time of year the water expresses itself or its essence most truthfully. As I stand beside a lake one winter day, I discover my image in the water staring back at me. A small, fleecy cloud passes overhead. Its reflection in the water touches my hair but does not disturb it. Instead, it seems to purify the water and my image still more. There I am, gazing fully at myself.

languishing snowman—

starlight falls

in flakes

❧THE SNOW has melted away but one resolute snowman stands in the naked garden. From the night sky flakes of starlight fall lightly over it as though attempting to preserve this solitary figure. But day by day, the snowman grows smaller. It will remain, a sentinel, watching the approach of spring to this garden until the very last bit of itself shall have disappeared in the sunlight or starlight.

❧A MOONLESS SKY ripples in the starlight. Perhaps the language of the stars is their very light. They are so distant from one another, so alone and lonely, that I think they must speak to each other and to the things on earth. White lilies are meditating in the silent darkness of my garden until they touch the ancient starlight kindled two hundred thousand light-years ago. This mingling of serene starlight and white lilies must be one of the most astonishing and awesome scenes which heaven and earth together create. It seems more beautiful than beauty; more mysterious than mystery.

the star two hundred

thousand light-years distant—

lilies touch the light

❧THE HUSTLE and bustle of a busy autumn day fades into pale dusk. An evening bell tolls over the village. Wild geese fly with a cry toward the mountains. Then darkness fills the space completely between earth and sky. The flock of geese disappear among the stars. Lamps go out in house after house along shadowy streets. Silence deepens in the starlight; solitude deepens in the silence.

the starry sky

swallows up

wild geese

the sun

departed and sent

stars to the lake

❧FAR OFF on the horizon the sun has set. Afterglow tempers the sky. Cool night breezes rise up from the west and rustle dry leaves on the oaks. Autumn scents the air. I stand on the shore of a little lake, but strangely enough, the lake is making small lapping waves from its own drops of light. The sun secretly surrendered bits of its light to the lake, and it is alive with rocking stars.

stars'

reflections

stir the water

❧I AM STANDING by a little lake. Its surface is rippling; the water is starry. I wonder whether it is the water moving or the stars. The deeper the darkness, the brighter the reflections of the stars. I ponder this delicate communion between earth and heaven, and cherish the mystery, taking care that it may not ever be broken.

❧DUSK COMES SUDDENLY to the glen in autumn. It arrives with a feeling of crisp coolness. The sky, aglow with a setting sun, bursts into stars. A little brook passing by seems dusky, too, yet is sensitive and transparent enough to mirror the stars themselves. All through the night, the brook reflects these murmuring stars streaming down through a cloudless sky.

autumn brook:

murmuring stars

are streaming

❧IN AUTUMN, the air becomes crisp and clear. Even lakes and streams seem more lucid and transparent. Now a mountain stream has joined a swift-moving rapids. As the stream recovers from the tumult, it flows quietly and smoothly onward. The water becomes clear as glass. I can see stars reflected whole again after their broken flurry over the rapids. Both water and stars portray a lovely harmony under the clear, nocturnal sky.

gentle stream:

broken stars

become whole

shooting star

showers sparks—

crickets' cries

A SHOOTING STAR streaks across the sky, scattering sparks. Crickets burst out crying. They must be feeling some violent burning, for their cries become more shrill. In a few moments, the star disappears and the crickets' voices soften. Then the darkness increases and silence settles back heavily. All things, animate and inanimate, on earth and in the sky, must be connected by an invisible string of feeling.

cherry blossoms—

lightning claws

the darkness

IN THE MIDST OF SPRING, cherry blossoms are in their full glory. But even in springtime, nature is not always tender and cannot keep cruelty hidden. Now a thunderstorm rages in the darkness as though the dark itself was the storm's own weapon. Rain hits the flowers heavily. Trees cry in the wind. Thunder rolls over the hills and fields. The talons of lightning tear at the flesh of night. Flowers are seen trembling through the cracks of darkness each time the lightning flashes.

IN MY NATIVE VILLAGE, most homes had their own wells. At my house, a deep well lay in the garden. Its water was very pure and tasty. In the winter, it never froze, and the water was at its clearest. So were the stars that I drew up from the well with each bucket full of water. I, as a child, was deeply moved with this starry water. It truly seemed as if I were drawing up stars. Today, most of these wells have disappeared, but buckets full of stars still twinkle in my eyes. This beauty, fostered in childhood, will never fade away. A lovely thing *is* a joy to behold forever.

the winter well:

a bucketful

of stars

A WATER LILY unfolds in fragrant sunshine just offshore. The water, holding the blue sky above, recedes somewhat from this first lily in order to lend it dignity. Perhaps tomorrow, after this introduction, other water lilies will open and glorify the summer with their pearly whiteness.

in scented sunshine

a lily unfolds

offshore

lightning

dispels the darkness

over roses

❦NIGHT FALLS like a curtain over the garden. In this darkness, roses have all lost their form and color. But still a faint sweet smell floats on the air. I sense that the roses are breathing. From the distance come rolls of thunder. In a sudden brilliant flash, lightning discloses the full bloom of the roses. Then just as swiftly, darkness descends again over the garden. For one moment, lightning and darkness have become one to reveal a delicate, poignant beauty.

thunderstorm over,

the moon gleams in each raindrop

gathered on green leaves

❦A THUNDERSTORM that had raged all afternoon is finally over. As evening deepens, a full moon appears in the quiet sky. Perhaps the moon had driven the storm away. I stand transfixed at the sight. The moon appears to be lulling and caressing all things after the violence of the storm. Then I turn my eyes to the wet grass at my feet. I see the moon shining in each raindrop collected on the green leaves.

●THE CHIMNEY of the crematory is belching smoke. Her body is burning into ashes. People stand silently watching the rising smoke. The air at the foot of the mountain turns colder. Her countenance spreads across the winter sky as the smoke vanishes moment by moment. Is this the absolute end of her life? No, I assure myself. Her being will never disappear within me. Everything of her will be a flower in my garden.

cremation:

smoke vanishes

into the winter sky

●IT IS THE TIME of winter solstice. A peaceful silence gathers, and I sense a response to all those prayers being breathed forth from the hearts of the devout. The flicker of the candle-glow reveals the countenance of the Christ figure. This light on the darkest night of the year awakens in me a deep and very clear sense of being and of the eternal.

the winter solstice—

candlelight throws into relief

Christ's countenance

lightning's claws

tear the flesh

of night

LIGHTNING sharpens its claws. Blood vessels of the darkness itself are revealed in its brilliant flashes. The lightning turns more ferocious. Claps of thunder punctuate the deepening darkness. As the lightning approaches me, it tears away the flesh of night with its claws, and from the open wounds a bloody rain falls heavily upon the earth. I have a long way to go in the storm.

lightning's claws

tear the flesh

of night

THE CALM fostered by a perfect day is broken by the onslaught of a stormy night. Each time lightning flashes, the darkness is split in two with a deafening crash; the ground quakes; the air shatters. In that moment of flaring impact, an uncanny sight is revealed. A white butterfly climbs a crack in the darkness as though it were soon to be sucked up by the lightning flash itself. Yes, the butterfly is approaching the fiery streak. Does its soul seek such violent passion?

streaks of lightning;

a white butterfly climbs

the crack in the dark

a shooting star

tears the dark:

a rain of sparks

A SHOOTING STAR carves a long curve in the night sky. The darkness is torn apart with silent screams. Sparks rain from the crevice gaping in the dark. It is a dreadful scene but not without beauty as the terrifying light and the darkness perform together in the fractured sky for several moments. Even after the scene has perished, the image burns hotly in my mind.

outside the sickroom—

a cricket ceases chirping;

the sound of footsteps

A LONESOME SPIRIT of autumn has scented the dusky air. I lie in bed, ill, day and night. On one particular evening, the voice of a solitary cricket singing outside the house enters my room. Its shrill voice penetrates my mind. Suddenly, the chirping stops. Everything is wrapped in heavy silence. Then another sound is heard. I sense someone approaching and guess from the footsteps. It is a friend of mine. So it is that different sounds touch my fragile heartstrings to make music deep inside.

On summer mornings, I go to the mountains to enjoy a symphony played by nature. Summer mountains produce a variety of lovely sounds: birdsong, deep-throated arias of frogs, the rush of streams, the rhythmic splash of waterfalls, the whisper of winds, and the rustlings of green leaves. These sounds together form a harmonious whole in the refreshing morning air. After washing the mind with such a symphony, I return home.

summer morning:

mountains play

a symphony

A wind-bell rings to show that the wind is blowing. When there isn't any wind, of course, it doesn't ring. It is sensitive enough to catch the faintest trace of moving air, and it changes its tone quality according to the intensity of movement. My wind-bell is tinkling now. So is my neighbor's. The two sounds touch each other and create delicate shades of coolness that drift into my room.

the wind-bell's song

touches another:

variegated coolness

the darkness

swallows fireworks

one bloom after another

❧A FIREWORKS DISPLAY has begun on the river. Numberless people have gathered to gaze skyward at this nocturnal event. As the fireworks split the darkness, one colorful flower after another blooms but vanishes in a moment. These are the most short-lived flowers in the world! A shout of joy arises on earth. Momentary beauty intoxicates human hearts so much. When the display is over, certain questions arise in my mind: Are fireworks the stimulus needed to open the darkness to flowers? Is it really fireworks that bloom in the sky? Might the darkness have its own flowers within itself?

digging potatoes

potato families

turn up

❧VEGETABLE GARDENING is very interesting. For instance, in spring I plant potatoes in a corner of my vegetable garden. In late summer, I dig them out. At this time, I'm surprised and happy to see how the potato families have grown. Each now contains several children of various sizes, plump parents, and wrinkled grandparents.

☙MOUNTAIN ASHES which have turned red are reflected in a placid lake. Nothing disturbs the solitude. Suddenly, the blast of a shotgun shatters the air. the report bounces across the water causing the red reflections to tremble. Simultaneously, an image of the shot spreads over the lake. Pieces of broken silence sink to the bottom where they are stowed away.

red mountain ashes:

gunshot explodes

over the lake

☙THE SETTING SUN has disappeared over the horizon, but a last ray of light floods a lone persimmon left clinging to the highest twig of a tree. The flaming orange-red fruit, an offering to the goddess of fruitfulness, glows in splendor. The leafless tree stands like a shadow against the darkening sky. Somewhere a shrill voice weakens the wind.

dusky fields:

sunlight stays

on a persimmon

the autumn sun—

ears of rice are nodding

to a farmer

🖋AUTUMN has fully ripened. The countryside unrolls in rich pastoral cadences beneath an azure sky. Fields of golden rice sway in the sunshine while composing, it seems, some idyllic poem. Even the wind is gentle with them. Nearby, a farmer smiles at the shiny paddy fields. Ears of rice nod back at him. Both rice plants and the farmer's thoughts blend in peaceful harmony.

the typhoon is gone;

evening fields

stand silent

🖋AN OMINOUS CALM preceded the storm. After sunset, dark clouds appeared, the wind came up, and rain fell heavily. The storm raged throughout the night. But when day broke, a new sun dissipated the clouds and quieted the wind. It also revealed severely spoiled gardens and vineyards. It seemed winter was stealing over these fields once so profuse in vegetation and now drained of their energy.

☙IT IS LATE FALL. After a rain the air is calm and cold. The road through the village is pitted with puddles. Despite the muddiness of the water, I see the moon mirrored clearly in each puddle. The image in no way appears inferior in beauty to the moon in the sky. On the contrary, I observe that the muddy water has been able to catch and hold this beauty of the heavens here on earth. Musing on this, I experience the "muddiness" of my mind clearing away, and things around me revealing their beauty clearly.

muddy water

mirrors moon

as it is

☙AN EARLY BLIZZARD is raging through the woods so intensely that plants and animals can hardly catch their breath. Trees are writhing in pain, their voices rending the air. Winds whirl the biting snow about faster and faster, and the stinging, whirling snow encourages the wind to persevere in its violent attack. Leaves cling for their very lives to the branches of the trees.

the blizzard:

leaves are clinging

to writhing branches

a little wind

whirled away the butterfly

from my garden

SPRING IS WELL ADVANCED. The flowers in my garden are full of color: yellow, red, blue, white, pink, and purple. New leaves smell sweet. Bees and birds come and go. Yesterday three butterflies bestowed their particular charm upon the garden. Today only one butterfly is playing among the flowers. Suddenly, a little whirlwind disturbs the calm and sweeps the butterfly away in a single instant. The flowers are left shaking. But after a little while, tranquility reigns once more over the pleasant garden.

a little wind

whirled away the butterfly

from my garden

A WINTER WIND brings clouds up from the west. Darkness gathers, and a penetrating cold sets in. With sharp claws the heartless wind tears at the darkness, shredding and compacting the freezing pieces and blowing them away as snowflakes into the frosty air. Wind, clouds, darkness, and cold have combined to create a snowstorm this chaotic night.

the wind tears

darkness into pieces:

a snowstorm

the nipping wind:

the movements of grass and light

are frozen

❧THE WIND makes the air colder. As it blows across the dry grasses, it sighs and moans even louder. The sun has lost everything except its light, and even this will be frozen soon. When the brittle grasses cease their bending in the wind, they, too, will freeze into silent, motionless spires. Flakes of sunlight begin fluttering down like diamond dust. In this coldest of seasons, there is much beauty to behold.

the storm is over—

the ground is littered

with rosy apples

❧A LATE EVENING STORM visited the countryside. Heavy winds fanned the rain. The driving rain, in turn, fanned more wind. Leaves flew wildly through the air on the screams of the trees. Darkness was torn to shreds. Thus the storm raged furiously all night long.

But now the morning sun has dissipated the storm, exposing all the damage of field and forest. A farmer stands quietly in the mayhem, gazing at the ground littered with rosy apples.

THIS MARCH DAY seems exactly like a spring day. The air is comfortably warm. Nothing in the sky or on the earth supports the illusion these premature signs might convey. The very next day, a blizzard is under way, depriving March of the spring that had just begun to grow; crushing all buds swelling in human minds.

the blizzard

deprives infant March

of a little spring

ALL IS FROZEN. Even sounds are frozen. I am afraid I shall freeze in this winter loneliness. I look around. Trees are standing still in the snow. Grass is lying quiet under the snow. Then to my ears comes a voiceless voice: "Nothing meets spring without going through winter." I begin to walk again, wondering what lies beyond this frozen world.

a frozen world:

nothing speaks

to me

a frozen path:

stones are shrouded

in white

❧THE SUN seems to have lost its power to melt the frozen things around me. Stones on the roadside lie covered in white as though shrouded for death. Of course, the stones have no power in themselves to melt their frozen pall. At any moment, I, too, may be frozen in this whiteness. Such a thought chills my bones. I, too, would be unable to melt my frozen self.

summer wind

sleeps

exhausted

❧AT MIDDAY, the room lies in sweltering heat. The moment a little wind enters the window, it becomes motionless. It, too, is quite exhausted and in an instant lies fast asleep in the room. As I ponder these things, I find I cannot move at all. If I move, I might tread upon the wind. When evening comes to cool the air, then the wind will awaken and leave.

♪NIGHT HAS DESCENDED. A biting wind blows through the deserted street. As I walk along, a sharp metallic sound reaches my ear. I approach the sound with curiosity. I see a mason working with stone. He works alone, striking the stone with rhythmic drives of his hammer. His whole heart and soul seem thrown into this work. With each blow, fiery sparks burst from the stone. The mason's burning eyes appear in the momentary fracture of darkness. They seem to mirror his very soul, breathing life into the stone. The steady ring of his hammer is like a reflection of the mason's song making this moment beautiful.

the frosty night:

a mason's eyes

stare at sparks

frozen darkness:

someone knocks

at my heart

❧ONE WINTER AT MIDNIGHT, I awoke at a sudden sound. I strained to make it out. Someone was knocking at the door. I got up and went to open the door but found no one there. "It is the sound of the snow," I thought. But after entering the room, the sound of knocking came again. I stood still beside the door, wondering who or what it might be. I could not identify the sound. Then I noticed myself becoming cold to the bone. I lit a candle in haste and made a fire in the stove.

a plane

drills

the frozen sky

❧THE WINTER SKY is beautifully blue. A lake, which isn't frozen over yet, reflects the brilliance. The day itself seems to be performing a symphony in blue. While I am gazing upward, an airplane comes into sight. It looks like a giant drill. It is not flying but drilling the transparent frozen blue sky, leaving white noisy chips behind. Products of our modern civilization can be so destructive to both earth and heaven.

It was a windy winter night. The moment I stepped out of the house, I was amazed to see beautiful snowflakes glistening in the moonlight, fluttering in the strong wind. As the flakes rushed about me, I could hear a tinkling sound like breaking glass. "What is this?" I wondered. Then I thought, "The wind is breaking the frozen moonlight into pieces." It was a momentary truth. Because I was so intoxicated with the manifestation of this winter beauty, I could not separate the snowflakes from the moonlight flakes.

glittering flakes:

the wind breaks

frozen moonlight

Fallen leaves are trampled underfoot during the day. After sunset, the wind, which has become stronger and more capricious, tosses them into the air. Having become quite worn and tattered, they lie exposed to a pelting rain, and the autumn chill nips them relentlessly. There is no rest even for fallen leaves.

the evening wind:

fallen leaves

have no place to lie

morning window:

the sun scatters

diamond dust

❧ONE MIDWINTER MORNING, I awoke to a delicate, strange sound. I got up and drew the curtain back in haste. Brilliant flakes were fluttering on the air outside my window. I stood gazing in rapture at the glittering display. Was this diamond dust or ice crystals? Excitement surged within me. I said to myself, "This is the finest work of art I have seen displayed by nature in this northern country. It is the coldest season of the year, yet such superb beauty continues to exist." This thought warmed and brightened my heart all winter long.

❧ONE WINTER rose blooms in the garden where all other flowers have faded away. This red rose gives life to the desolate garden, yet appears to be wringing out the last drop of lifeblood before it, too, dies. The day soon comes to an end. Sunshine perishes and the air turns cold. Clouds gather. Dusk deepens around the winter rose. It stiffens with the approaching night.

a winter rose—

the evening sun

remains no more

a white bud

on the lake opens

into a swan

✿THE AIR IS CHILL. A hesitant sun begins to shine on the rippling lake. As the day grows, the sky turns an intense blue, startlingly clear after a night of multi-colored northern lights. Silence is undisturbed. The lake is dotted with small ripples resembling small white buds. The blue water and white buds form a delicate and pleasing contrast to the eye. As the rippling effect continues, a beautiful spectacle unfolds on the lake: white buds open into one large, encompassing swan.

a white bud

on the lake opens

into a swan

✿A LAKE IS ENCIRCLED by virgin woods. No movement disturbs the lake. All is covered with the gray stillness of early dawn. A pair of sleeping swans nestle close together. Then, as the first faint streaks of light whiten the sky, the swans lift their voices in song. The sound reverberates across the lake, pushing back the silence until the entire lake is revealed. Having regained its life, the water ripples in the morning sunlight. Trees, flowers, and sky sway in brilliant reflection.

swans sing

in the first light;

the lake opens

fading cries

of wild geese:

the void deepens

🖙WILD GEESE are flying away, moving off in a line, their cries fading away with them into the dusk. The heavens are suddenly very silent and empty. This void filling earth and sky, resonates in the lonesomeness felt in the autumn evening. Such a parting inscribed in the human mind will not easily be erased!

a kite squeezes

melodious sound

from the freezing air

🖙A KITE flies alone in a sky aglow with the setting sun. But the cold grows more severe and snowflakes flutter like diamond dust to the ground. People are making their way home. The wind scatters a melodious sound over the withering fields as the kite squeezes through the freezing air on its return journey to earth.

❧AN EVENING SUN shines dimly over the mountains. Soft snowflakes begin to fall. A crow caws from a treetop, its hard voice echoing on the air. An old man plods silently along the road, his bent figure becoming more and more blurred as the snow thickens. The crow sharpens its voice and the cold intensifies. Both earth and sky are joined to enrich this wintery milieu.

the winter sky:

a crow cries,

"cold! cold! . . ."

❧THE AFTERGLOW of the sunset is about to fade. Clouds gather as a wind picks up. The air turns colder and freezes the rural landscape. The trembling voice of a stray crow is heard as it seeks warmth and shelter from winter's onrush. Visual, tactile, and acoustical sensations of winter are expressed in this scene.

the evening glow:

a crow's voice trembles

with cold

out of the moon

a carp jumps

into the air

🖙THERE IS SOMETHING so attractive about the moon and we each respond differently to it. As I look down at the moon reflected in a pond, it is being colored by my particular feelings. The water is so clear and calm that the moon's reflection is nearly perfect. Suddenly, a carp breaks the surface, jumping into the air and diving back down again. The moon's reflection is smashed to pieces. But after a few moments, the pond becomes as smooth as glass again and the pieces of full moon are all fitted back together.

snow peak—

moss pinks

waving at the base

🖙THE TOP of the high mountain is still covered with snow. But the snow is diminishing as the sun grows warmer day by day. Moss pinks in bloom are waving and winding themselves about at the base of the sprouting mountain. Each color— pink, green, and white—is brought into prominence amid the fragrant sunshine to create a picturesque composition of springtime.

WHITE LILIES are blooming in the fields. Their orderliness and clarity stand out among the green grasses. I turn my eyes to the distant mountains. Into view appear majestic snow-covered peaks. While I am feasting my eyes upon this scene, brilliant under the summer sky, a sound reaches my ears. It seems to me that the two whitenesses, the lilies and the snow, are reverberating, one against another. The lilies, I decide, may be embodiments of the mountain snow which has melted and run off. If so, they may be pining for their former being.

white lilies in fields

re-echo

snowy mountains

TO THE WEST of town rises a mountain, its peak covered with snow. This evening the snow is shining with the glow of the setting sun. The snow-covered mountain seems to be swallowing the flaming sun. Around me, scarlet drops of sunlight fall. Thus the boundary between winter's night and day is marked with a showy beauty of red on white. I feel a flame burning within myself despite the rigors of the season.

a snowy mountain

is swallowing

the flaming sun

chick peeps

flutter among dandelions

stretching to the lake

🖊THE WHOLE FIELD is ablaze with dandelions. A breeze drifts across the lake. Small yellow chicks are not seen from where I stand, but their chirping voices are heard moving about among the dandelions. Earth and air abound with new life. So congenial are the sun, sky, grass, flowers, and trees that this balmy spring day grows more mellow until all is flooded with peace and warmth.

the dawning sky—

blackbirds scatter

the scent of lilac

🖊AT THE FIRST MOMENT of dawn when night touches day, blackbirds start to sing. Their trill rises as the voices of other small birds add to the song. Amid this lightsome chorus, the darkness of night completely disappears and flowers unfold in the growing light. The fragrance of sweet-smelling lilacs is borne upon melodious breezes. It is at this precise instant between night and day when most people are asleep that the drama of spring reaches its zenith.

❧THE ROUGH SEA is gulping down a bloody sun. Its waters foretell the coming of a storm. But the sky is not showing such indications at all. The sea breaks and sends up a spray of the setting sun over a tiny fishing village almost lost beneath the winter snows. The shower seals icicles to boats and eaves. Not a fisherman is to be seen. The village glows like an ember stirred by the wind.

the sea outpours

the setting sun—

a snow village glows

I sweep and sweep,

still snowflakes

fall on me

🕊FROM OUT OF A HEAVY, cloudy sky snowflakes are falling steadily. "All will be buried under snow," I think as the field of white broadens and deepens both on the earth and in my mind. I sweep and sweep the snowflakes off myself, but they never stop falling on me. I walk on in the endless snowy world. If I stop walking, I may not be.

I sweep and sweep,

still snowflakes

fall on me

🕊A PAPER CRANE is lying on my desk. Summer has passed into autumn and the air is comfortably cool. Through the open window moonlight enters my study on a gentle breeze. Suddenly, the paper crane stirs and stretches its wings as if full of life. It appears that it is going to fly away. The crane is true to its nature, and it is the chilly air, consecrated with moonlight, that contains miraculous power.

cool moonlight:

the paper crane

is ready to fly

a moon

is fished up—

darkness tightens

❧ AT TIMES, the moon seems to be brought or "fished" up by some invisible string. At such times, the atmosphere feels tense. As the darkness tightens, so does my mind. I wonder, "Why does my mind do this?" What string is this? Who is pulling it? Does someone set this stage for the night?" I cannot find any definite answers. In this world there are many more things we cannot understand than we do understand. But I believe this predicament enriches human life.

a pebble

smashed a moon

to pieces

❧ ONE AUTUMN NIGHT I stood beside a pond. I watched a cloud hug the moon, then drift away. I suddenly picked up a pebble and threw it into the water. I do not know what made me do so. In the next moment I cried, "Oh, I have made a mess of it!" The moon was broken to pieces and scattered about on the disturbed water. Then, after collecting the moon together again, the pond lay slightly trembling.

THE LAKE is frozen over. The ice glistens silvery in the moonlight. No sound breaks the stillness and peace of this winter night. I do not even feel the cold amid such scenic beauty. Suddenly, a simple idea occurs to me. I pick up a pebble from the shore and toss it out onto the ice. The pebble rolls across the frozen lake, uttering a small cry. The cry thins and disappears into the distance. Clouds come out of the silence and cover the full moon.

moonlit evening:

a pebble rolls on the ice

uttering a cry

I WALK DEEPER into the long winter night. A north wind penetrates my body. Darkness lies heavily on my mind. Above, a crescent moon cuts its way into the frozen darkness. I am walking with the moon now but I still have a long way to go; a very long way of winding and wandering over the snow. There is no light but the moonlight; no sound but the wind.

a crescent moon

cuts its way deeper, still deeper

into the frozen dark

falling snow:

nothingness to nothingness

my footprints go

❧THE WINTER SKY is very cloudy and gray. The wind begins to blow. Soon frozen snowflakes are falling everywhere. As I walk hurriedly along, my footprints vanish in the snow. I consider that I may be losing my way in the storm. "The snow will bury me," I think. "But to stay here will bring certain death. I must go on walking with a more focused consciousness of all existence moving from nothingness to nothingness."

under duckweed

lies a moon

of gold

❧ONE NIGHT as I opened my curtain, mellow beams of the moon streamed into my room. I was so fascinated that I went outside to stroll around a nearby pond. I stopped for a while to get a good view of my surroundings. I happened to push away some duckweed from the surface of the water and discovered a full moon hidden there. This moon was even more beautiful than the one glowing in the sky.

•

*THE SNOWSTORM is gone. No sound is heard over the expansive white darkness. I set my mind at ease, allowing my thoughts to wander playfully. Suddenly, a point of light on the horizon brightens. I catch sight of a huge golden bud slowly rising above the earth. I watch with wonder as a full moon transforms the forlorn and desolate winter night into a world of resplendence.

the snowy prairie:

a bud on the horizon

swells into a moon

*THE HOUSE where I spent my childhood stood on a hill about three miles from the shores of the Pacific Ocean. At one corner of the garden there was a deep well from which I often drew water—and moon-light—with a wooden bucket on a rope. This bucketful of moonlight touched me deeply. So now, the beautiful image of bygone days is mirrored in my mind's eye. Memories turn and swirl about the well. Sometimes I still draw water and moonlight from it and make a rainbow from the drops of water to fill my empty cup.

from the well

I draw a bucketful

of moonlight

morning rain

taps on trees:

bud, bud, bud . . .

WINTER IS OBSERVED departing and spring arriving as snows melt and ice grows thin on lakes and streams. Cold temperatures abate, and, day by day, fields and hills slowly become green. Even the bark on naked trees brightens. Now the first spring rain gently falls to recolor the earth, rousing all from sleep. The rhythmic tapping of the rain encourages trees and grasses to put forth their buds. And they respond: bud, bud, bud . . . The air itself resounds with the breath of life.

morning rain

taps on trees:

bud, bud, bud . . .

lotus flowers:

scent of moonlight

is changed

⚘THE MOON hangs serenely in the night sky. The air is cool. Lotus flowers are open. The clear moonlight seems to intensify their simplicity and purity while the blooms, in turn, enhance the clarity of the moonlight. Along a stairway of moonlight, the sweet scent of lotus flowers climbs silently to the moon. All is hushed. Even a breath would break the tranquillity of this event. Nature is ever occupied in revealing her profound ways through color, form, smell, touch, and taste.

the shower's gone—

the Seine flows

gathering moonlight

⚘AN EVENING SHOWER is over, having washed the city of Paris. Streets are wet with brilliant moonlight. The summer night lengthens, creating a quiet mood. Neon lights flicker multi-colors silently. I walk along the streets, coming finally to a bridge over the Seine. But I am stopped as I cross the bridge by sudden intense moonlight flooding the river. It is a transformation of beauty created by the evening shower, and an unfathomable movement of nature.

THE MIST at the top of the mountain thins and clears. Then an awe-inspiring spectacle greets me: a brilliantly blue summer sky; mountain ridges standing rank upon rank; a lake gleaming far below; cattle and sheep grazing peacefully on grassy slopes. But at my feet lie clusters of star-shaped edelweiss growing among the small stones and in the shade of rocks. Could these tiny white flowers be incarnations of the mist?

into rocks

the mist vanishes;

edelweiss appears

THE DAY IS DONE. Birds have gone to rest. An evening mist has wrapped the mountains with the sound of silence. Suddenly, the mist clears like a curtain being drawn away. A cloudless night sky, sprinkled with glittering stars, is revealed. In one single moment, the appearance of the mountains has changed, exhibiting another beauty. This panoramic tableau is sustained until daybreak.

a faint sound:

the mountain mist clears

into stars

a raindrop—

irises' reflections

are shaking

🔹A SINGLE RAINDROP touching the water ripples the lake and the reflections of irises tremble. A whole shower of raindrops ensues. When the rain is over, the clouds depart. A little wind remains, reluctant to relinquish the mood of the hour, and each raindrop left suspended from the leaves of grass reflects within itself an image of the trembling irises. The reflection is caught motionless now. Repose amid motion; motion amid repose.

rain

permeates

cicadas' cries

🔹IT IS RAINING in the mountains at midday. The sound of the rain penetrates the sharp chirp of cicadas calling for heat. Without losing their furious vigor, their cries pierce rocks and trees and leaves, enveloping the entire mountains. Why are these vocalists singing so loudly? Are their hearts burning so hotly, so madly for love?

When cherry blossoms open in the spring, their beauty lasts only briefly; either the wind blows or the rain falls to scatter the delicate flowers. But I have observed distinct differences in the rain falling upon these flowers. Some rains fall hard; others gently. As I watch the rain fall on the cherry blossoms now, I hear a softer sound as if the hearts of the flowers were moving the rain more deeply.

cherry blossoms—

the sound of the rain

falls milder, still milder

Bibliography

Anderson, Harold H., ed. *Creativity and Its Cultivation.* New York: Harper & Brothers, 1959.

Chamberlain, Basil Hall. *Japanese Poetry.* London: John Murray, 1910.

Fussell, Paul. *Poetic Meter and Poetic Form.* New York: Random House, 1979.

Giroux, Joan. *The Haiku Form.* Tokyo: Charles E. Tuttle, 1974.

Hearn, Lafcadio. *Kotto and Kwaidan: The Writings of Lafcadio Hearn.* Vol. 11. New York: Houghton Mifflin Company, 1922.

Higginson, William and Penny Harter. *The Haiku Handbook: How to Write, Share, and Teach Haiku.* New York: McGraw-Hill, 1985.

Horiuchi, Toshimi. *Synesthesia in Haiku and Other Essays.* The University of the Philippines Printery, 1990.

Keene, Donald. *Japanese literature: An Introduction for Western Readers.* Tokyo: Charles E. Tuttle, 1984.

Lewis, C. Day. *Poetry for You.* Oxford: Basil Blackwell, 1961.

Lewis, C. Day. *The Poet's Way of Knowlege.* Tokyo: Nan'undo, 1986.

Minot, Stephen. *Three Genres: The Writing of Poetry, Fiction, and Drama.* Englewood Cliffs, N. J.: Prentice Hall, 1971.

Nakagawa, Atsuo. *Studies on English Haiku. Tokyo:* Hokuseido Press, 1976.

Noguchi, Yone. *The Pilgrimage: A Book of Poems.* London: Elkin Matthews, 1909.

Perrine, Laurence. *The Art of Total Relevance.* Rowley: Newbury House Publishers, 1976.

Stevens, John, trans. *Mountain Tasting: Zen Haiku by Santōka Taneda.* New York: Weatherhill, Inc. 1989.

Yasuda, Kenneth. *The Japanese Haiku.* Tokyo: Charles E. Tuttle, 1978.

More Poetry by Toshimi Horiuchi

Drops of Rainbow (1979)
A Broken Music and Other Stories (1982)
Minnesota Songs (1982)
Journey to the Fire Flower (1990)
Synesthesia in Haiku and Other Essays (1990)

About the Author

Born in Fukushima Prefecture, Japan, in 1931, Toshimi Horiuchi graduated from Tohoku Gakuin College and later went on to study Creative Writing and American Poetry at Saint John's University, Collegeville, Minnesota, and British and Irish Poetry at Exeter College in Oxford. He is currently a professor of English at Sendai Shirayuri Junior College, Japan.

The "weathermark" identifies this book as a production of Weatherhill, Inc., publishers of fine books on Asia and the Pacific. Editorial supervision: Cynthia Di Martino. Production supervision: Bill Rose. Book and cover design: Liz Trovato. Printing and binding by Quebecor/Fairfield. The typeface used is Minion.